555 Powerful Questions for Leadership, Coaching, and Mentoring Today

555
Powerful
Questions for
Leadership,
Coaching, and
Mentoring
Today

Mastering Effective Questions to Unlock Potential, Enhance Performance, and Empower Teams in the Modern Workplace

Be.Bull Publishing Group
Mauricio Vasquez
Toronto, Canada

555 Powerful Questions for Leadership, Coaching, and Mentoring Today by Be.Bull Publishing Group (Aria Capri International Inc.). All Rights Reserved.

Authors:
Mauricio Vasquez
Be.Bull Publishing Group

First Printing: June 2024

ISBN 978-1-998402-56-4 (Paperback)
ISBN 978-1-998402-57-1 (Hardcover)
ISBN 978-1-998402-58-8 (Ebook)

Dear Valued Reader,

We kindly ask for your support in leaving a review for our book. Unlike large publishing companies, we rely heavily on the feedback of readers like you.

Your review will not only help us improve and reach more readers, but it will also allow you to share your insights and experiences, contributing to a community of like-minded individuals who are passionate about leadership and personal growth.

To leave your review, please scan the QR code provided.

Your input is invaluable to us, and we thank you in advance for your support!

Warm regards,

Mauricio Vasquez
Be.Bull Publishing

INTRODUCTION

Asking questions is, has been, and always will be a fundamental part of our nature. Questions allow us to gather information, learn new things, and strengthen our relationships with others uniquely.

Why is asking powerful and insightful questions crucial for your work and life?

Foremost, asking questions and truly listening to others shows you genuinely care. When you are at work and ask powerful questions to your colleagues, they will know that you value them and their needs and opinions. Your interactions will always be more successful and gratifying when you are honest and intentional in acknowledging their needs, knowledge, and perspectives.

Asking questions lets you align your organization's goals and strategies with your colleagues' objectives, priorities, and needs, and vice versa. This alignment requires understanding and empathy towards others. While you might have a general sense of what your colleagues expect from you and your company, including their goals and needs, understanding these accurately is not always straightforward.

What if you are making wrong assumptions and hold false beliefs? As a result, your words and actions might not align with what your colleagues think and feel. This misalignment can lead to ineffective relationships and poor performance.

Although the value of powerful questions is widely acknowledged, how often do you pose meaningful questions to your colleagues and teammates? What questions are you asking? Are you using the right terminology? Are you asking too many close-ended questions? And finally, are you using the answers to strengthen your relationships and help others improve their awareness and performance?

If you ask questions and do nothing with the responses, what is the point? It can create the opposite result of what you are trying to achieve. Asking questions goes far beyond exchanging information.

Here is a quote I find very relevant to asking the right questions:

"The tough thing is figuring out what questions to ask, but once you do that, the rest is really easy." - Elon Musk.

There is no need to develop counterproductive questions or spend hours figuring out the much-needed powerful questions. I have done all the heavy lifting for you.

This book has 555 powerful coaching, mentoring, and business leadership questions. This book will help you ask questions—and particularly, asking the right questions that will draw out insightful answers — answers can help you transform your business.

By embracing these questions, you will not only improve your leadership and decision-making but also foster stronger, more meaningful relationships within your organization. This book aims to equip you with the tools to navigate the complexities of modern leadership, coaching, and mentoring, enabling you to achieve remarkable results.

GUIDELINES FOR ASKING POWERFUL QUESTIONS

Unlocking learning and improving performance starts with asking the right questions. Dive into these engaging guidelines to master the art of powerful questioning.

- **Effective questions are open or focused, depending on the context:** Open-ended questions that cannot be answered with a simple yes or no are the key to evoking deeper thinking and reflection. Tailor your questions to the situation to broaden awareness and stimulate learning.
- **Effective questions support learning:** Aim to stimulate thinking and deepen your colleagues' understanding. Your insightful questions should focus attention on the most valuable aspects of the issue at hand, guiding your team toward meaningful insights.
- **Effective questions are asked for the benefit of others:** The primary goal is to stimulate your colleagues' thinking and enhance their understanding. Remember, it's not about you—it's about facilitating their growth and comprehension.
- **Effective questions engage a personal response:** Results are driven by people, and your role as a leader is to engage them on a personal level. Invite responses that reveal how they feel and what emotions they bring to the situation. Personal responses to challenges or choices are powerful catalysts for learning.
- **Effective questions look beyond problems to future outcomes:** Shift the perspective from problems to solutions. When a colleague is entangled in an issue,

impactful questions will open new opportunities for action and growth by focusing on future outcomes.

- **Effective questions facilitate openness versus defensiveness:** Frame your questions with a non-judgmental tone and open body language to encourage openness. Avoid starting questions with "why," as this can elicit defensive responses. Instead, use language that fosters a safe and open dialogue.
- **Effective questions co-create best options versus manipulating outcomes:** Aim to co-create solutions with your colleagues rather than leading them to what you think is best. If you have a suggestion, offer it directly instead of disguising it as a question. This encourages authentic and collaborative problem-solving.
- **Less is more:** Simplicity is key when it comes to powerful questions. Ask one question at a time and avoid long-winded, complicated inquiries. Short, simple questions like "What is that all about?" or "What will the consequences be?" get straight to the core and encourage profound reflection.

By mastering these guidelines, you will transform your questioning technique, enabling you to unlock deeper learning, enhance performance, and build stronger connections within your team. Embrace the power of effective questions and watch your leadership, coaching, and mentoring flourish.

TIPS FOR THE USE OF THIS BOOK

With these practical tips, you can maximize the impact of "Book—555 Powerful Questions for Leadership, Coaching, and Mentoring Today." Leverage the power of effective questioning to unlock deeper insights and foster meaningful conversations.

- **Reference Versatility:** We've organized questions into different chapters based on their type, but feel free to use this as a reference. Many questions can apply to multiple categories, offering flexibility in your conversations.
- **The Power of Listening:** The cornerstone of any meaningful conversation is listening. Pay attention not just to words, but also to emotions, body language, and energy. This holistic approach will help you connect more deeply with your colleagues.
- **Tailor Your Questions:** Customize questions to fit the conversation and the person you're engaging with. Tailored questions resonate more and lead to more impactful discussions.
- **Combine for Depth:** Don't hesitate to mix and match questions to delve deeper into the topic. Combining questions can help you uncover layers of insight that single questions might miss.
- **Options for Creativity:** Some questions include a couple of options and a blank space for you to add your own twist. Use this flexibility to spark creativity and make the questions uniquely yours.
- **Follow-Up for Clarity:** Follow-up questions are essential for diving deeper. They help clarify responses

and uncover what truly matters, leading to a more profound understanding.

- **Adapt to Your Style:** Make the questions your own by adapting them to your vocabulary and communication style. This personalization will make your conversations feel more natural and authentic.

- **Keep It Simple:** Ask one question at a time to avoid overwhelming your conversation partner. Short, simple questions are often the most powerful, cutting straight to the issue's core.

By applying these tips, you'll be able to harness this book's full potential, facilitating richer, more insightful conversations that drive growth and understanding in your leadership, coaching, and mentoring roles.

TABLE OF CONTENTS

Accountability

1. How can you enforce your sense of accountability towards (yourself/your responsibilities/your team)?
2. How can you help yourself stay accountable to your (goals/commitments/project deadlines)?
3. What can you do to be more fully present with your (colleagues/supervisor/team members)?
4. How do you want to hold yourself accountable for your (actions/performance/decisions)?
5. Who can you ask to hold you accountable for achieving your (objectives/targets/commitments)?
6. How would you like others to hold you accountable in your (role/tasks/projects)?
7. What is the plan to keep yourself on track with your (goals/commitments/tasks)?
8. What strategies can you implement to help yourself be more courageous in your (decisions/actions/interactions)?
9. What do you want to acknowledge yourself for in terms of your (achievements/contributions/growth)?
10. What relationships can you leverage as an accountability measure for your (goals/tasks/commitments)?

Action

11. What actions will you take towards your (purpose/learning goals/professional development) this week?

12. What specific actions are you prepared to take to get (new clients/customers/partners)?
13. What is the plan for you to achieve your (objectives/competitive edge/targets)?
14. What is the next step to complete your (business plan/marketing strategy/project)?
15. What is there for you to (manage/control/oversee) to ensure success?
16. How do you manage your (suppliers/subordinates/team) to maintain efficiency and quality?
17. What have you tried so far with (investors/contractors/stakeholders) to improve the situation?
18. What will you do differently at work based on what you have discovered about (yourself/others/your team)?
19. What do you need to do less of to get closer to your (quota/team objectives/goals)?
20. What is the most important (task/project/initiative) to act on now?
21. What is the first step you want to take to reduce (variable costs/outstanding payments/operational expenses)?
22. What should you continue to do to maintain a healthy relationship with (colleagues/suppliers/clients)?
23. Which factors are most vital in taking a (proactive approach/bold step/strategic initiative)?
24. How can you inspire yourself to shift your viewpoints to find new opportunities for action?
25. How can you achieve the accomplishments you want for your (future/career/goals)?

Awareness

26. What are you becoming more aware of about yourself and your (work/work ethic/role)?
27. What do you love about your (role/position/current responsibilities)?
28. What do you secretly dread about your (work/position/current responsibilities)?
29. What is true for you right now about your (job prospects/professional progression/career path)?
30. Where are you over-invested or under-invested in your (work/tasks/commitments)?
31. What would you like to get out of this (exercise/experience/situation)?
32. What is clearer now about your (priorities/competencies/areas of focus)?
33. Who are you becoming when you are being (selfish/mindful/reflective)?
34. What is your current reality regarding your (role/tasks/overall situation)?
35. Are you currently in a down-spiral or a positive mindset regarding your (work/role/professional life)?
36. How is the (mission/vision/strategy) of the company influencing your pattern of thinking?
37. When you say you are not ready, what image or picture comes to your mind?
38. What image or picture do you see in your mind when you talk about the (value proposition/pain points/goals) of the company?
39. Where are your ideal self and real self different?
40. What questions do you have about the (culture/mission/values) of the company?

41. What are you becoming more aware of about (yourself/your team/your role)?

42. How can you continue to stay aware of the impact of your thoughts on your (responsibilities/role/performance)?

43. What do you want to acknowledge yourself for regarding your contribution to the (company/team/project)?

44. What do you imagine is going on here?

45. What is at stake if you don't reach your (sales target/key performance indicators/strategic goals)?

46. What is required to help you raise your awareness of underlying (beliefs/assumptions/mindsets)?

47. How can you raise your awareness about the (beliefs/assumptions/mindsets) you are operating with and the consequences of operating with them?

48. How can you help yourself notice your emotions, both the ones you express and the ones that lie beneath what you are saying?

49. What (meaning/interpretation/perspective) are you placing on your team's feedback?

50. What new awareness do you have because of not achieving the desired (outcome/solution/result) you had in mind?

51. What is missing from the (action plan/process/strategy)?

52. What do you notice about the (client/yourself/situation)?

53. What assumptions have you made in the past that were proven to be false?

54. How can you uncover any internal and external obstacles in executing your (actions/plans/strategies)?

55. Where are your ideal and real selves different in your (professional/personal) life?

Belief

56. Where are you in balance or out of balance with your (workload/commitments/responsibilities)?
57. What are the pieces of evidence for your thinking about the (business plan/strategy/current approach)?
58. What are counter-evidences for your thinking about the (business plan/strategy/current approach)?
59. What beliefs do you have that empower you to finish your (goals/commitments/tasks)?
60. What beliefs do you have that disempower you from fulfilling your (goals/commitments/tasks)?
61. How do your (beliefs/work ethic/assumptions) shape your actions?
62. What beliefs or assumptions about yourself are being challenged?
63. What assumptions are you making about the (situation/audience/project)?
64. What is it about the (situation/challenge/task) that could give you the outcome you want?
65. How well does the belief that you hold about the (issue/problem/task) serve you?
66. How helpful is it to you to believe that your work can't (improve/change/evolve)?
67. How helpful is it to you to believe that work should always be fair?
68. How helpful is it to you to believe that there is another way of looking at the (issue/problem/situation) that might serve you better?

69. How helpful is it to you to believe that there could be a different outcome in terms of how you feel about the (issue/problem/challenge)?

70. What disturbs you most in your (work/role/environment)?

71. What do you have to lose if you pursue this (path/goal/strategy)?

72. Who are you at your best?

73. What beliefs or assumptions are you making about (yourself/others/your situation)?

74. Where do your assumptions or beliefs limit you?

75. What are the implications of your (proposal/responses/actions)?

76. What beliefs about work prevent you from moving forward?

77. How else can you think about your (behavior/attitude/approach)?

78. How can you shift your underlying (beliefs/assumptions/mindsets)?

79. Who do you want to become in your (career/life/role)?

80. How do you know the (proposed solution/proposed timeline/plan) works?

81. What don't you believe today that you believed to be true a long time ago?

82. What are your perspectives on your (responsibilities/motivation/goals)?

83. What if you really believed that you could change your (career/performance/life) by changing your choices?

Challenge

84. Where do you want to go with the (thought/conversation/project)?

85. How can you motivate yourself to do something that is outside of your (comfort zone/routine/regular tasks)?

86. What is a new challenge you want to work on in your (role/career/project)?

87. What aspects of the (situation/project/task) need to be clarified more?

88. Where are you off–track in your (career/project/efforts)?

89. What gets in your way of achieving your (goals/tasks/objectives)?

90. What do you need to do differently to be a more positive influence on your (teammates/clients/colleagues)?

91. What choices do you make about your own (identity/professional image/personal brand)?

92. In what ways does your (negativity/mindset/attitude) serve you?

93. What else do you see when you encounter a (problem/difficulty/challenge)?

94. What will be the process to help you move into a different frame of reference?

95. What data can you select that could refute your assumptions?

96. What are you being challenged by with (public speaking/team projects/new responsibilities)?

97. What will be more challenging for you than your current (role/responsibilities/tasks)?

98. What do you see as the obstacles in your (way/professional life/career path)?

99. What will you do about the (challenge/obstacle/issue) you are facing?

100. How do you best navigate through a (challenge/obstacle/difficult situation)?

101. How do you best adapt to a new (challenge/position/role)?

102. How do you best thrive in a new (role/position/environment)?

103. What strengths can you draw on to help you deal with the (challenge/project/task)?
104. What internal resistance do you have to taking action?
105. What about now?
106. How can you help yourself see things from a different perspective?
107. What gets in the way of your progress?
108. What was an experience where you took a risk and it paid off?
109. What is the limit of your comfort zone?
110. What impedes your (goals/work/progress)?
111. What alternative view is there for you to look   at on the (situation/argument/issue)?

Change

112. How can you help yourself shift to a more effective (mindset/approach/attitude)?
113. What do you need to do to improve (customer service/defect rate/process efficiency)?
114. Where in the (sales process/client service process/workflow) are you most stuck?
115. What did work about the (situation/project/strategy)?
116. What did not work about the (situation/project/strategy)?
117. What would it be like if the (challenge/problem/obstacle) were solved?
118. What can you change in your (approach/strategy/process) to address the current challenges?
119. What would you do if you wanted to change your (work routine/attitude/habits)?

120. What would be the impact if you do not change your (work/routine/approach)?
121. How will the changes you make affect your (goals/outcomes/professional growth)?
122. What would you do if you wanted to change your (work routine/attitude/approach)?
123. What would be the impact if you do not change your (work/routine/behavior)?
124. What shift in (thinking/attitude/strategy) do you need to make?
125. What do you need to let go of to move forward?
126. Where are your areas of continued development?
127. What is the change you want to see in (yourself/the team/the organization)?

Commitment

128. What will have to happen for you to act on your (responsibilities/vision/commitments)?
129. What are you responsible for in the upcoming (prospecting meeting/team meeting/presentation)?
130. What are you committed to (achieving/sharing/implementing)?
131. What will you put in place to support your (commitment/work/objectives)?
132. What do you commit to do to get a (promotion/salary increase/new opportunity)?
133. How committed are you to move forward with the new (project/responsibilities/initiative)?
134. How are you going to hold yourself to the commitment regarding your (tasks/goals/deadlines)?

135. How can you stay in control of your (workload/schedule/priorities)?
136. What do you want to do as a (next project/role/initiative) at work?
137. How can you discover more enjoyable ways to accomplish what you need to accomplish in your (work/tasks/responsibilities)?

Creativity

138. What do you want to do as a (next project/role/initiative) at work?
139. How can you discover more enjoyable ways to accomplish your (tasks/responsibilities/goals)?
140. What lines of questioning or paths of exploration would you take for (yourself/your team/your project)?
141. What do you have when your creativity is unleashed in your (work/role/projects)?
142. What connections do you see between your (performance/habits/approach) and your (fulfillment/balanced scorecard/achievements)?
143. How would you describe your (role/contribution/impact) to others?
144. What is important about being creative with (others/your team/your clients)?
145. How do you create a relationship of trust with (yourself/clients/team members)?
146. What is the value of accessing your creative (source/mindset/potential)?
147. How do you connect with the source of your creativity in your (work/processes/tasks)?
148. How do you connect with the source of your creativity in your (work/tasks/projects)?

Decisions

149. What is a realistic time frame for you to accomplish your (performance goals/tasks/objectives)?
150. How do you manage your (time/prioritize tasks/schedule) effectively?
151. What new possibilities for action do you see with your (team/supervisor/colleagues)?
152. What is going to be most important to you about the decision to (rescind/join/pursue this opportunity)?
153. What do you most want from the decision to (rescind/join/accept this role)?
154. How does your choice to (take part/join/participate) allow you to express your values?
155. What are you willing to do to (win market share/build volume sales/achieve your targets)?
156. What will you focus your (energy/time/efforts) on moving forward?
157. How are you bringing yourself to (work/team meetings/collaborative efforts)?
158. How can you better balance your open mind and critical reflection to make the best choices you could make?
159. How are you bringing yourself to (work/team meetings/projects)?

Excitement

160. How do you best develop yourself in your (career/profession/role)?

161. What excites you the most about (management/leadership/your current role)?
162. What do you feel most energized by in your (work/daily tasks/projects)?
163. When you have a (promotion/salary increase/new opportunity), what will that give you on a deep level?
164. What would make your (work/relationships with others/team dynamics) more satisfying for you?
165. In what situations does your energy go up?
166. What would be the reason for your energy going (up/down/fluctuating)?
167. In what situations does your energy go down?
168. What energizes you in your (work/tasks/interactions)?
169. When do you need different pacing compared to your usual pacing?
170. What is deeply satisfying from the experience of being with your (coworkers/customers/clients)?
171. How do you best take part in your (work/projects/tasks)?
172. What are the environments that bring out the best in you?
173. When do you feel most energetic and fulfilled at work?

Fear

174. What are your concerns about the (culture/growth plans/strategic direction) of the company?
175. What could get in your way of achieving your (mission/dreams/targets)?

176. What is scary about the new (roles/responsibilities/tasks) for you?
177. What concerns, fears, and/or questions do you have when setting goals for yourself?
178. What most upsets you about your (work/role/responsibilities)?
179. How can you avoid being discouraged due to fear or lack of faith in yourself?
180. What is becoming clearer about your place in the (company/team/organization)?
181. Where are you allowing your inner critic to run the show in your (work/personal life/professional development)?

Feelings

182. Whether you are setting goals or just defining a sense of direction, what will it feel like when you reach them?
183. What do you need to do to be more (empathetic/understanding/supportive) towards others?
184. How can you become more aware of what is contributing to your feelings in your (work/personal life/interactions)?
185. How do you feel about (change/stress/new challenges)?
186. How does your (team/manager/work environment) make you feel?
187. What is your attitude towards (work/goal setting/professional development)?
188. What is your mood towards your current (work/performance/role)?
189. What is significant for you about today in your (work/life/schedule)?
190. How would you feel if you could get a (promotion/job transfer/new role)?

191. What are you feeling as you face the (situation/challenge/task)?
192. What are you feeling as you learn about your (opportunities for improvement/potential/challenges)?
193. What does your (work/profession/career) mean for you?
194. What is the impact of the (issue/problem/situation) on you?
195. How is your (role/team/organization) influencing your feelings or mood?

Flow

196. Where do you choose to focus primarily in your (work/tasks/responsibilities)?
197. What is the common theme running through the things that you do well and with a sense of flow?
198. What is the 'thing' you are always motivated to do, and that shows up in all your most energizing, fulfilling experiences?
199. How can you experience more flow in your (work/responsibilities/projects)?
200. When working on a (project/task/assignment), what would be the determinant for you to push forward or take some time to consolidate and integrate?
201. How does your inner self-processing system influence how you navigate through your (work/tasks/challenges)?
202. What is your optimum state of being at (work/home/your tasks)?
203. How can you access your optimum state more often?
204. How can you help yourself access your optimal self when dealing with your daily (responsibilities/problems/tasks)?

205. Think about a specific moment in your life when you felt deeply engaged or fulfilled, what made such a moment special?

Fulfillment

206. What makes work (meaningful/boring/rewarding) for you?
207. Who are you in your (role/profession/career)?
208. Who do you want to be in your (professional/personal) life?
209. What holds you back from becoming a more fully realized person?
210. What do you need to develop in yourself to be your own hero?
211. What do you need to do to become a super (boss/leader/mentor)?
212. What are the things that provide you with fulfillment at work?

Goals

213. What is your most important purpose nowadays in your (career/role/professional life)?
214. What is the first idea that comes to your mind as your professional purpose?
215. Whether you are setting goals or just defining a sense of direction, how will you know when you reach them?
216. When you reach your (learning goals/performance goals/career milestones), what will that give you?
217. What tends to distract you from your (goals/objectives/priorities)?
218. What is the goal that, if you achieve it, will make other things much easier?

219. How can you use your strengths to help you achieve your goals?
220. How might you go about achieving your (goal/target/aspiration)?
221. What goals should you continue to focus on?
222. What new goals have emerged in your (role/professional journey/career path)?
223. What are the most important tasks that you would like to achieve this year?
224. What do you need to achieve your (target/goals/objectives)?
225. Where are you now relative to what you want to achieve?
226. What is the learning goal that will move you closer to achieving your performance goal?
227. When you reach your fulfillment goals, what will you have?
228. What goals would you like to set for your (career/personal development/team)?
229. What is next for you in terms of development?
230. What do you really want to achieve?
231. What kind of accomplishment do you want for your future?

Habits

232. What do you consistently end up (doing/thinking/focusing on) no matter what the context is?
233. What (role/task/responsibility) do you consistently seem to be attracted to, independently of the environment?
234. What would you like to try next to reduce your (errors/miscalculations/inaccuracies) in your reports?
235. What external obstacles could impede your targeted (deliverables/cash flows/goals)?

236. How might you get in your own way of becoming a more fulfilled (professional/leader/employee)?
237. How can you broaden your current (perspective/thinking pattern/approach)?
238. What is a recurrent pattern in your career?
239. What habits do you need to (change/improve/develop) at work?
240. When do you stop listening to your (colleagues/clients/team members)?
241. What is the impact if you are fully present compared to when you are not fully present?
242. What do you feel would make your (work/tasks/projects) more effective?

Learning

243. What are you learning about (yourself/your team/your role)?
244. What are you taking away from the (experience/project/assignment)?
245. What could be the reason for your energy going down?
246. What does not work well and could be a significantly missed opportunity?
247. How can you keep exploring and connecting your thoughts to counteract the inner critic that shuts you down?
248. How is that shaping your (beliefs/assumptions/perspectives)?
249. Are you aware of what did not work well in your (approach/strategy/effort)?
250. What is a significant missed opportunity in the last year?
251. Do you have a sense of how you would do it "better" if you could have the opportunity again?

252. What are you now curious about in your (work/field/profession)?
253. What are you learning about yourself as you progress in your (role/project/career)?
254. What are you seeking now to grow yourself?
255. What did you learn about the (situation/project/task) that worked?
256. What did you learn about the (situation/project/task) that didn't work?
257. What can you learn about your (colleagues/clients/team)?
258. What would be a learning opportunity related to your (performance/work/skills)?
259. What are some critical variables that you think may be useful to observe when you (work/contribute/collaborate) with others?
260. What can you learn about yourself from a successful (priority/task/project)?
261. What have you learned from previous (roles/projects/experiences)?
262. What was the missed opportunity?
263. What has worked well for you when working with your (team/supervisor/colleagues)?
264. What has been least beneficial?
265. What else would you like to learn?
266. How have your (failures/successes/experiences) contributed to your duties and work?
267. What are the new areas in your professional life where you want to become more effective?
268. What has been the biggest lesson from a recent (success/failure/project) in your professional life?
269. What was a great lesson that you learned in a tough moment in your professional life?
270. What did you learn from the last time that you failed?

271. What was something that you sacrificed that has given you something even better?
272. What has (surprised/challenged/inspired) you recently?
273. What did you learn from something that has challenged you recently?
274. What was a situation in your life where you wish you could have done something differently?
275. What did you learn from a situation in your life where you wish you had done something differently?
276. When can you find more insights about (yourself/purpose/goals)?
277. What has been one of the most positive learning experiences about yourself at work?
278. What did you do right when you faced a challenge where you took a risk and it paid off?

Listening

279. What kind of conversation would you have with yourself to move the (acquisition/project/initiative) forward?
280. What is the missed opportunity when you don't do your best at work?
281. What failures did you experience on the pathway to those successes?
282. What impedes (listening/helping/understanding) others?
283. How can you better help yourself identify where you are most stuck in a (project/problem/task)?
284. How can you get better at listening?
285. How can you prevent harmless things from affecting you in the future?

Mindset

286. What is there for you to appreciate about (successes/failures/challenges)?
287. How is your own state affecting the relationships with your (supervisor/subordinate/team)?
288. How does your (work/environment/role) limit you?
289. What is stopping you from acting on your own (priorities/ideas/initiatives) now?
290. What are your criteria for (success/failure/progress)?
291. How well do your (beliefs/mindset/assumptions) serve you?
292. How can you prevent harmless things from affecting you in the future?
293. What mindset are you choosing for yourself today?
294. What questions can you ask yourself to raise awareness of the mindset you are operating with?
295. What are the conditions in which you feel most comfortable (at work/when working with colleagues/in your environment)?
296. What are you more curious about in your (work/team members/role)?
297. How will you feed your curiosity?
298. What is possible in your role?
299. Where would you rather be than in your current position?
300. What is unique about the (opportunity/role/project) you have?
301. Who are you professionally at your best?
302. What if you really believed that you could change your results by changing your choices?

303. What are you actively pursuing in your profession?
304. What do you most want from the (experience/challenge/opportunity)?
305. What are you trying to accomplish?
306. What purpose is being served when you are trying to accomplish the goals of your (team/company/department)?
307. How can you encourage more self-observation?
308. What are you prepared to do to move forward?
309. How do you best survive in difficult times?

Options

310. What are your choices to deal with a potential (bankruptcy/economic crisis/major setback)?
311. What is your choice right now regarding your (career/path/decision)?
312. How will you approach the (obstacle/goal/challenge) ahead?
313. What do you see as the opportunities in the (project/problem/situation)?
314. How will you approach the (problem/meeting/situation) if you see it as an opportunity?
315. What is another perspective on the (plan/commitment/strategy)?
316. What is right about the (experience/project/initiative)?
317. What new possibilities do you see for improving the (situation/task/project)?
318. What is more important for you between stability and challenge in your (career/role/decisions)?
319. What will make the biggest difference in the (project/plan/strategy)?

320. What options appeal to you in your (current situation/role/project)?
321. What prompted the choice of selecting your current (role/position/career path)?
322. What has been working when you make your choices?
323. What hasn't been working when you make your choices?
324. What would you like to improve about (yourself/your team/your approach)?

Performance

325. What resulted from your efforts on your (top priorities/goals/projects) last year?
326. How have your results on (team projects/tasks/initiatives) moved you forward professionally?
327. What led to the (budget deficit/closure/challenges) of your department?
328. How do you feel when you do your best work?
329. What would be an ideal outcome for (you/your business/your team)?
330. How can you facilitate change in yourself that will lead to your desired (results/performance/outcomes)?
331. How could you overcome what is blocking you from reaching your potential?
332. What can you do (better/faster/more efficiently)?
333. What do you commit to doing to improve your (relationships/performance/skills)?
334. What goal, if not acted on, might have the biggest negative impact?
335. What needs to (be different/change/improve) for you to achieve your performance goals?

336. What do you feel you have most benefited from working here?
337. What would the process for improving your (performance/results/productivity) look like?
338. What are you most proud of in your (work/career/achievements)?
339. What would you like to improve about (yourself/your team/your work)?
340. What values can guide your own development toward realizing your potential?

Preferences

341. What do you pay attention to in your (work/role/daily tasks)?
342. How do you choose what to pay attention to in your (work/role/priorities)?
343. How do you define (success/failure/achievement) in your (work/role/profession)?
344. What do you like about your (work/role/responsibilities)?
345. What would you do if you knew you had very limited time left to complete your (projects/tasks/goals)?

Priorities

346. What do you need to stop doing to be more productive in your (work/tasks/role)?
347. What is your experience of managing multiple (priorities/goals/projects) at the same time?
348. What is your highest priority at work?
349. How will you prioritize your goals in relation to the other (tasks/projects/responsibilities) you have been working on?

350. What is most important to you about the (company/company's culture/team environment)?

351. What is the priority now in your (work/role/projects)?

352. What do you really want to achieve in your (career/role/current project)?

Progress

353. What does (winning/progress/success) mean to you?

354. What needs to change to improve your (well-being/mental health/work-life balance) at work?

355. What signposts do you recognize in your own (learning/change/development) process?

356. How can you celebrate your successes?

357. What are the possibilities when you do your best?

358. How are you different now compared to when you started working with the company?

359. What steps are involved when you set plans for (success/improvement/growth)?

360. What can you put in place to track your (progress/performance/development)?

361. How do you feel about your progress when trying to reach your (goals/targets/objectives)?

362. How satisfied are you with your pace of progress?

363. What is one accomplishment that you are very proud of working hard to achieve?

364. What are the best ways you can stay on the path to your (development/progress/goals)?

Purpose

365. When you reflect on your professional life, what's the recurring theme or common thread?
366. What is your vision for yourself within the (company/team/organization)?
367. What do you now better understand about your (purpose/priorities/goals)?
368. What is essential to you about 'being on purpose' in your (work/role/life)?
369. What is the emotional connection you have with your (purpose/mission/vision)?
370. What do you want to achieve with your (team/department/project)?
371. What is the (goal/objective/milestone) you'd like to achieve?
372. How will you know when you achieve your (intention/goal/desired outcome)?
373. What will you do if you fail in achieving your (desirable targets/goals/objectives)?
374. What are you willing to do to fulfill your (purpose/goals/commitments)?
375. What do you want in your (career/role/life)?
376. Who do you want to be in your (profession/organization/life)?
377. What do you want to have in your (career/life/profession)?
378. What contribution do you want to make to the (company/team/organization)?
379. What is your purpose in your (work/career/life)?
380. Where are you aligned with your purpose?
381. What gives you a sense of purpose in your (work/career/role)?
382. What do you understand now about your purpose?

Relationships

383. How have your recent (successes/failures/efforts) affected others?
384. What is important to you about the support from your (leader/manager/team)?
385. Whose responsibility is the (project/task/initiative)?
386. What brings you fulfillment when working with (colleagues/clients/partners)?
387. What could be your contribution to creating more trusting, open relationships with (suppliers/clients/stakeholders)?
388. How can you find out what works well in interactions with others?
389. How do you frame your duties in relation to the rest of your team?
390. How can you develop supportive and trusting relationships with your (colleagues/clients/team members)?
391. What are you learning about yourself in your relationships with others?
392. What types of people are you drawn to in your (work/personal life/professional network)?
393. What does it mean for you to be fully present and fully yourself with (others/clients/team members)?
394. Where do you give away your power in relationships?
395. What is the nature or quality of your presence when you are fully present?
396. What is the nature or quality of your presence when you are not present?
397. What gets in the way of you being fully present?
398. What are the triggers that typically have you "shrink back" in an interaction?

399. How do you best contribute to your team?

400. What is important about being with your (team/colleagues/clients)?

401. What is important to you about sparking ideas with others?

402. Who else needs to be involved in your (project/initiative/task)?

403. In what way do others need to be involved in your (projects/tasks/initiatives)?

404. How will you involve others?

405. What would be your advice to a colleague who is concerned about you?

406. What is a relationship at work that you should improve?

407. What would be the first step you should take towards improving the relationship with your (client/colleague/manager)?

408. What kind of quality do you want others to see in your career?

409. What do you bring to relationships with (clients/colleagues/team members)?

410. What would you choose to do if you wanted to be an active and contributing member of the (team/company/organization)?

411. What supports you in being fully present at team meetings?

412. What fuels your passion for work?

413. What resources could you access to face any obstacles at work in a more fulfilled way?

414. What support or resources do you need to do your work better?

415. How can you help yourself develop long-term resourcefulness?

416. What resources do you have available to help yourself move forward?

417. What structures do you need to put in place to have more patience with yourself?

418. What new (habits/behaviors/routines) will support you best?

419. How can you develop or change to serve you better?

420. How can you become more aware of your (feelings/emotions/thoughts) that are involved in the situation you are exploring?

421. What tools do you need to develop to give yourself the confidence to better deal with your (responsibilities/targets/goals)?

422. How can you access your own power to create the career you want for yourself?

423. What does it take for you to access your self-trust?

424. What tools do you have to inspire yourself?

425. When you notice you are not being fully present, how can you bring yourself back?

426. What contributes to meaningful (responsibilities/roles/tasks)?

427. What resources could you access to assist with your work?

428. What resources do you need to better support your (team/manager/department)?

429. What are your most precious resources?

430. How can you use your current resources for whatever you are now facing?

431. What structures do you have available to help you?

432. What would you do if you had unlimited time and resources?

Self-Assessment

433. What led you to say your (comments/accusations/observations)?

434. How will you take the first step to improve (professionally/your presentation skills/your leadership skills)?

435. When will you take the first step to improve (professionally/your presentation skills/your leadership skills)?

436. Where are you now relative to where you want to be professionally?

437. Who are you at your core?

438. What makes you unique in your (role/profession/industry)?

439. What are you passionate about in your (work/career/personal development)?

440. What professional (successes/failures/lessons) have you experienced recently?

441. What did you learn from recent (successes/failures/challenges)?

442. How has your perspective on your (responsibilities/potential/goals) changed over time?

443. What led you to say your (comments/accusations/feedback)?

444. How can you be more self-observant?

445. How can you gain deeper insight into what you desire for the future?

446. How will you measure progress?

447. What is truly essential to you in your (work/company/career)?

448. What did it take for you to accomplish the one thing that you are most proud of?

Skills

449. What is the gap in your skills between your current reality and your desired future?
450. What new skills do you need to add in order to reach your (performance indicators/cost reduction targets/strategic goals)?
451. What skills energize and inspire you as you use them?
452. How have the skills that energize and inspire you changed over the years?
453. What is the best route for you to gain a new skill?
454. Where is your highest leverage in applying your skills?
455. What new skills do you want to develop to become more effective in your (role/tasks/projects)?
456. What skills do you already have that you can use in pursuit of your (goals/key performance indicators/strategic objectives)?
457. What are the (skills/qualities/attributes) required to create collaboratively?

Strategies

458. How can you acknowledge yourself for your (courage/commitment/dedication) even if you fail in your strategy?
459. What are possible strategies for achieving your (key performance indicators/cost reduction targets/goals)?
460. What could get in the way of you taking the required steps to complete your (forecast/budget/project)?
461. How can you experiment with new (behaviors/thoughts/approaches)?

462. What (strategy/plan/approach) will be most effective and/or efficient?
463. What new (strategy/plan/approach) will fit in with the reality of your current situation?

Strength

464. What strengths of yours come into play when you face exhilarating challenges?
465. Considering your life in the last 5 years, which are the top three to five strengths you have used in that period?
466. What comes easy to you?
467. Taking into consideration the (role/task/responsibility) you consistently seem to be attracted to, what does that tell you about your strengths?
468. Has your (passion/joy/enthusiasm) for using a particular strength increased or decreased over the years?
469. Is there any strength or set of strengths that feels especially right for you?
470. When you look at your list of strengths, what patterns do you see?
471. What are your inner (gifts/talents/skills)?
472. What are your strengths?
473. What are the pieces of evidence of your strengths in your career?
474. How strongly do you own your strengths in your (role/position/responsibilities)?
475. What are you noticing about your own strengths in your (work/performance/interactions)?
476. How will you know when you are using a strength effectively?

477. How do you intend to work with your strength in your (current role/future projects/team)?

478. What tasks or activities will be easy for you due to your strengths?

479. What are the assets from your past that you can leverage in the future?

480. What happens when you are using one of your strengths?

481. Considering your strengths in your (goals/objectives/targets), how do your strengths serve you?

482. How could you use your strengths to move you forward towards your (goals/objectives/targets)?

483. How can you learn to notice how your strengths show up in your (work/responsibilities/tasks)?

484. When do you push your strengths to their extreme?

485. What is the impact when you push your strengths to the extreme?

486. How do you know when you push your strengths too far?

487. What are some unintended consequences of your strengths?

488. What is the impact of your strengths on others?

489. When are you tempted to hide your strengths under a shade?

490. What strengths do you have that you no longer enjoy using?

491. Where are you pretending a strength where there isn't one?

492. How can you leverage your strengths more effectively?

493. How good is the fit between what your (role/position/job) requires of you and your actual strengths?

494. What is the impact of the misalignment between your role and your strengths?

Support

495. What can you do to prevent making an incorrect (assumption/action/decision)?

496. How can you support yourself to stay focused on the (big picture/task/project)?

497. What can you do to provide yourself with a self-confidence boost?

498. What will move you forward towards desired (results/sales/outcomes)?

499. What structures does the company need to put in place to support (you/your work/your team)?

500. What support do you need to have available to have more patience with your (suppliers/customers/colleagues)?

501. What do you need to let go of in order to move forward more powerfully?

502. How can you put in place a new habit that will support you to achieve better (workflow/results/productivity)?

503. What alternative to your current (work schedule/work environment/process) can be constructed that would serve you better?

504. How can you better support your own (creativity/well-being/efficiency)?

505. What structures can you put in place to help you achieve the (project/goals/targets)?
506. What do you need to have to ensure you can move the (project/team/initiative) forward?
507. What support do you need to pursue your next new (client/employee/opportunity)?
508. What will you do to get the support you need?
509. What support do you need to take the first step?
510. How can you help yourself deal with (disappointment/setbacks/challenges)?
511. What is a challenge in your professional life where a new (structure/process/system) is needed?

Values

512. What do you value most in your profession?
513. What do you value in your (work/team/role)?
514. What are the values of the that represent you?
515. What values anchor you in who you are?
516. What values can guide your development towards realizing your potential?
517. What values guide you in creating and maintaining meaningful and productive relationships with (colleagues/clients/stakeholders)?
518. What is the most radical step you can take to honor your values more fully?

519. What can you change to honor your values more?

520. What small action can you take to be more in line with your values?

521. What are your values?

522. Where are you honoring your values in your (work/actions/decisions)?

523. Where are you not honoring your values in your (work/actions/decisions)?

524. How can you use your values to make better (choices/decisions/judgments)?

525. How can you use your values to design a fulfilling way towards a (goal/objective/achievement)?

526. What are the values and guiding principles that help you shed light on (challenges/problems/dilemmas)?

527. How else can your values be honored in your (work/life/interactions)?

528. What is it costing you to continue ignoring your values in your (career/decisions/relationships)?

529. What is one small step you could take to live more of your values in your (daily routine/professional life/personal life)?

530. What are the reasons for the importance of what you value in your (career/life/relationships)?

531. What is the relative order of importance of your values in your (career/life/decisions)?

532. What values were you honoring in a moment in your life when you felt deeply (engaged/fulfilled/successful)?

533. What does it mean for you to act on what matters, given your personal values in your (career/decisions/life)?

534. What values can guide you in creating and maintaining meaningful and productive (relationships/collaborations/interactions)?

Weakness

535. What are the gaps in you (skills/knowledge/experience)?

536. What is the impact of your weaknesses on your (work/performance/role)?

537. What weaknesses do you need to work on to help you achieve your (goals/targets/objectives)?

538. How strongly do you own your weaknesses?

539. Where can you leverage your (weaknesses/strengths/skills) to improve?

540. What are your (weaknesses/gaps/areas for improvement)?

541. How can you give up familiar habits that generate (fear/anxiety/stress)?

542. How do your weaknesses get you into trouble in your (work/tasks/relationships)?

543. What is the impact when you don't improve your weaknesses?

544. What are some unintended consequences of your weaknesses in your (work/performance/interactions)?
545. What are the gaps in your (skills/knowledge/experience)?
546. What blind spots could you be missing in your (work/performance/interactions)?
547. What are your weaknesses in your (role/profession/skill set)?
548. What is the evidence of your weakness in your (career/performance/results)?
549. When you consider your non-strengths, which ones do you suspect will have a pay-off for you if you were to enhance them?
550. How do you know what kinds of weaknesses you are dealing with in your (career/work/skills)?
551. What is it costing you from not working on your weaknesses in your (career/performance/growth)?
552. Where are you pretending a weakness exists, where there is actually strength?
553. What will it mean to you if you can become really masterful at a current weakness you might have?
554. What can you learn or practice that will make you better at a certain weakness?
555. What (skill/competence/ability) do you need to gain to improve your performance?

Unlock Exclusive Resources for Enhanced Leadership
(EXCLUSIVE BONUS)

As a special bonus, we are excited to offer you exclusive access to **111 Follow-Up Questions** designed to deepen your conversations, clarify responses, and foster stronger connections with your team and colleagues.

These follow-up questions will help you unlock deeper insights and enhance your leadership effectiveness.

What You'll Gain:

- **Enhanced Engagement:** Keep your conversations going and show your genuine interest.
- **Deeper Understanding:** Gain clarity on responses and uncover hidden insights.
- **Stronger Relationships:** Build trust and rapport with your team through thoughtful dialogue.

Scan the QR Code to Access Your Free Follow-Up Questions:

Dear Valued Reader,

We kindly ask for your support in leaving a review for our book. Unlike large publishing companies, we rely heavily on the feedback of readers like you.

Your review will not only help us improve and reach more readers, but it will also allow you to share your insights and experiences, contributing to a community of like-minded individuals who are passionate about leadership and personal growth.

To leave your review, please scan the QR code provided.

Your input is invaluable to us, and we thank you in advance for your support!

Warm regards,

Mauricio Vasquez
Be.Bull Publishing

www.ingramcontent.com/pod-product-compliance
Lightning Source LLC
Chambersburg PA
CBHW031258120626
46545CB00007B/2870